Year of the Unicorn Kidz

Sundress Publications • Knoxville, TN

ISBN: 978-1-951979-27-0
Library of Congress: 2021950354
Published by Sundress Publications
www.sundresspublications.com

Editor: Erin Elizabeth Smith
Managing Editor: Tennison Black
Editorial Assistants: Kanika Lawton
Editorial Interns: Iqra Abid, Hannah Olsson, Saoirse

Colophon: This book is set in EB Garamond.
Cover Image: "Flower Garden" by James M Wine
Author Photo: Vaneyl Photography
Cover Design: Kristen Ton
Book Design: Erin Elizabeth Smith

Year of the Unicorn Kidz

jason b. crawford

Acknowledgements

Thank you to the lovely journals and magazines that gave space for my earlier drafts of these poems to exist and cultivate:

Cotton Xenomorph: "A Pantoum of Yellow Fields"

Empty Mirror: "Boystown" & "Beasts"

FlyPaper Lit: "PReP"

Four Way Review & *Gertrude Press*: Parts of "Debt"

The Lumiere: "A Duplex for the Boy with the Cool Blue Truck"

Poached Hare: "On Jukin' wit a White Boy"

Royal Rose: "Boys and Dress"

Spilled Milk: "Notes on Cruising the rest stop off exit 187 at 11:45 pm"

Split Lip Magazine: "Unicorn Kidz Dance under the Moonlight, too"

Thirty West: "Glisten"

West Branch: "The Art of Staying Alive"

Wussy Mag: "From the mouth of the Beehive" & "Unicorn Kid loses his horn"

"And because we didn't want our fathers to know," "The Last Fight I got into was over a Dr. Pepper," "In defense of boys being bois," and "Debt" all appear in *Good Boi*, the chapbook published by Neon Hemlock.

Table of Contents

Space

Reality

Forward

Some debts can only be paid with the body. And in jason b crawford's rebellious and desirous debut, a life is the cost of an errant belonging. Crawford shows that to exist outside of the paradigms of a racist and homophobic society, one becomes even more indebted to it. Blood is the price, token money, a down payment. The poems in this collection are full of everything a queer Black boi should and should not say, should and should not do—'i went where the boys found me irresistible and i made it out alive'—now what must be paid for that? Throughout this collection is the paranoia that the piper/the collector/the reaper will show at any minute. Yet, despite the foreboding, there is a precarious life that continues as it must.

Crawford wields the profane through the sublime beauty of poems that stage and provoke the most sensitive images that cause you to gaze and look away, flinching at your own dirty self. The voice hyper-aware of its embodiments, performing its perfunctory wants and traumas, presenting a personally codified self through delicately formed affects and revelatory turns of phrase. Though the desire that informs the text is obvious, what requires a closer examination are the other obsessions—presence, imagination, and the spectacles of life and death.

Poems such as 'The Last Fight I Got Into Was Over A Dr. Pepper,' 'and because we didn't want our fathers to know,' and the series of poems titled 'Notes...' may overtly explore these obsessions; poems like 'Unicorn Kid Comes Out to the Fraternity,' 'On Nights I Am In New York,' and 'A Pantoum of Yellow Fields' offer other subtleties which cause us to consider what motivates the insatiable need to witness, to participate, to exhibit—and how this need is configured through an identity threatened by society and causally preoccupied with violence, grief, and flesh.

Where this collection unmasks itself, revealing its layers of complicity and complexity is in the 'Debt' series which moves through registers of confession, rumination, and citation. The voice ever more lucid with its predilections:

    I think about the Grief I
have offered allowance, space at my table, a
good, warm meal.

Issues of lack and replenishment toggle through these series to critique how we understand our intertwined transactional natures, how our lives have become a series of exchanges:

    −in fourth grade, I liked a boy so much that I
only knew how to make fun of his shoes. A
year later, the same boy kicked dirt in my eyes
during recess and I thanked him.
and
    −I was once owned by a boy and all I received
in return was his guilt. Such a concept, the
property of lust. How we long so much to own
something[...]

and

–I cannot think of debt without thinking of
my own inheritance, of what has been gifted,
all of its costs. My mother's aching joints, my
father's temper.

Here, in these passages and forthcoming pages, is a brief glimpse into what is increasingly at risk—everything we must trade in order to have desire itself, everything that must go absent in order for us to be present, every exchange a barter with our life.

—Jonah Mixon-Webster, author of *Stereo(TYPE)*

The Etymology of Cruising

Before the Unicorn Kid

I.

a body found in the bottom of a

dumpster is

just that

        :::

      a body. ripped at its

      softest entrance.

        :::

a sack of skin with all of the faggot leaking out

        :::

charred,   maimed,   missing

    :::

to someone.

2.

In the time before

Grindr and gay bars,

men would crawl into

sharp spaces

between the teeth

of pining bark.

They would wait

and listen for shivering coats

in the hot pink night;

hoping for another

bushel to hide in.

3.

There's a man in the gym's new steam room
made of matches and dust. I am just a boy
who is looking for the quietest place to jerk
off. I have found many spaces of sopped sin:

the dim lit basement floor study room in
the University of Toledo library, the unused
showers on Lansing Community College's campus,
the bathroom on the third floor left

corner of the Arts and Sciences Building. But
this act of steam and sex seems to be my most dangerous.
How there isn't a door or curtain to
conceal me while I let my moist palm begin its

ritual. How the men look at me as fag/prey,
easily sponged by their willing hands.

4.

It's a simple head nod/glance where our eyes meet

:::

a foot's soft tap/clearing of the throat

:::

To say I have made space for you in me

5.

i watch my father sanitize the insides of a pig/as he prepares its body for our meal/slices down the middle of the stomach/stopping only at the sternum/the breaking of the rib/i see myself in this dripping animal/mangled and left strung up/to bleed out on the pavement/can only think of the boys/that have asked for my flesh to be delivered to them/the payment of my mouth or my cock or my blood soaking past their elbows/think of all the places i have left my body/how i'm still able to breathe and enjoy this meal

6.

See back in those days, all of
the glistening chapels of boys
were made of leather.

They would code the color of
their gagging desire in between
the licked pages of the bible.

Became filled with enough
cum to wash an entire pulpit of
stained glass men polished
again.

7.

The man finds me in the steam room like a
fresh young hog, ready to be flipped onto the

belly of the flame; how quickly he claimed me
to be his unwilling.
Rawhide clung

between the gap in his molars. Again
I feel so much like the dead. Feel
myself becoming.

8.

They find his teeth
a half-mile away
hushed in a pile of leaves.
I often wonder how many times
this could have been me. I do not know
when cruising began, but I do
find myself at the I-96 rest stop after leaving
my mother's house. I know I am not here
because I am lonely

or even for the wanting.

9.

Give me the ghost

Give me what is left of the cremating body

Give me the seared flesh stuck to the brick

Give me his eyes

The jaw of my lover

the only way I wish to remember him

Swallowing an entire field of dirt

Give me the park where they found him

and all of its grass

Give me the unstitching tongue

Give me back his smile

even if you have to pull it from

the cracked whistle of his throat

Time

"We feel around making sense of the terrain, our own new limbs, Bumping up against a herd of bodies until one becomes home"

Tracy K. Smith ~ "Us & Co."

Boys and Dresses

What is the act of playing with dolls
other than putting the boy in a dress?

What is the act of homophobia
other than ripping the doll from the boy's fingers?

What is this act other than calling your own kin
a faggot, removing him from every family photo?

What is to clock other than self—
—awareness of the time wasted in another boy's closet?

What is the humble snap other than a sharp reminder
of the sound the jaw can muster when hit?

What are the teeth but a new collection
of Polaroids clung to a growing boy's new body?

And what is all this if not the song of the boy
leaving, finding a new father in a man?

Is this not why we search for a daddy and cosplay
a man built like blood to choke us?

The boy takes his broken bits
and boils it all down into a warm bowl of soup.

Such a sweet offering, to give
the unknown sky our naked flesh so freely.

We take home ones that remind us of dad. We take
abuse like it reminds us of home.

Beasts

Everything that lives and moves about will be food for you
Just as I gave you the green plants, I now give you everything
~ Genesis 9 Verse 3

How we become animals:

What was here once
a body made entirely of straw
mouth, eyes, nails
painted in red
A doll given life
until ripped by the dog
Guts of hay and rotten fruit
decorating everywhere

    I thought this cruel
until I found it sport
To make a boy from clay
To make it dance in front of me

To tear it apart at the lungs

Finding feast became ritual

A new habit for me to swallow

Unicorn Kid Discovers Sugar

after sam sax

before i was certain of my queer
limbs and taste for spoiled

blood, i would often wonder
what bowls of sap my body

could fabricate. watched all the best
documentaries of flesh, slick

and colliding together like a roller—
—derby of hungry mountains.

every video seemed to consummate mouths
blooming of bone pearls jangling

in the bottom of the jaw, and i was always
curious of my body's ability to slush

out a graveyard. a small sanctuary
worth praying in. it was something i had to

figure for myself. the cum–stain sweat
of a man's velcroed tongue sharp

across my back. The salt pit we bury
deep in our gums, left to dry

like enamel frosting our plaqued teeth.
i did not have another body

to crack me open like a rotten egg.
a man with too many fingers pushing

against my chest until i was a furnace
spewing carbon. i learned this silt

on my own, back pressed against the cold
plaster upside down, feet wedged

into the corner of the wall. waiting
to be crystallized in my own

mist. often, i would miss, hit
my nose, my neck, my nipples.

but sometimes. if i could position
the body just right angle enough

i would acrobat directly
into the back of the soft palate.

didn't care much for the bitter film
dragging around my breath. yet i practiced

the wide open swallow
of liquid fist. tortured myself

in the name of filth. pried back
my organs and let the dust spill

out on my freshly washed shirt. licked up
the ash and pretended this wasn't just a sandstorm

blowing around my throat.

The Last Fight I Got Into Was Over A Dr. Pepper

For Ricardo's Bitch Ass

—and let the records show, I let him swing
first, it was wild-vined, heaved at my skull
like a rogue axe, missing the open field of my
right jaw, as I (not fully ducking but)
sidestepped out of his spiked fist's reach,
grabbed him by the shoulders and slammed
him across the locker room floor and he
didn't swing—

—until the third time I told him to do it,
only because I wondered if he truly would, if
under the lights of all these shiny new phones
and brooding smiled boys, he would become
a pro boxer, a wrestler, a Kung Fu master, the
clampering crowd egging on his confidence,
the annoying way he wanted to—

—be cool and I wanted to be cool and
nothing was cooler than a fight in the boy's
locker room where there were no teachers to
play barricade to our rushing testosterone

and how he would only pick fights with
everyone he knew he could find his body left
buried under—
—young boy queer and unknowing, placing
all his rage into his knuckles, I waited
patiently, poking at him with my words like
a stick, testing how macho his manhood was
in his chest and in his pants, but I couldn't do
anything until the first throw of closed palm
aimed at my nose like a scoped bullet, and I
just moved out the way, hands readied to
return his blood to the dirt—

and because we didn't want our fathers to know,

we hushed into the school-yellow locker room,
ran across three highways of basketball chatter
while men screamed at each other
over the court's jamboree of screeching new shoes,
something about the breaking of rules or laws
or the morality of hunger. We kept quiet
in the final row of benches, asked ourselves to bare
quivering palms, the soft beasts flicked on
by our tongues, the teaching,
oh, the teaching of being young. Simple wanting,
what anger we can stuff
in our jaws. Bent the body
into silver faucets.

There was the one time we were almost caught, the taste
of your flesh rancid in my mouth.

After that, every time I'd tell you
no one was in here,

no one would find us,
no one would even care,

I've been wrong before, I will be again.

Friends We Love

For Alex

What friends I have / / to open their palms to me / / and show the bed of roses / / left growing wild / / in the trenches of their veins / / Nightly / / I call them to say / / I survived another day but I was sad / / This to mean / / my body was left a discarded mess / / They are the first to know of my random hookups / / Would be the ones to know my death / / via the missing text back and Apple Location / / I listen as their words water me / / patch the sap dripping from my quickly dying skin / / I know they are the only sunlight I need / / to bask in it / / Alive / / petals full and growing / / towards them

On Nights I Am In New York

and my Love decides to Stay Home

i'm sure my love is
somewhere bellowing //
there is a hardy tune that
sits in his gut // if you
listen ripe enough you
will hear it // a thin
whistle passing through
the buildings from five
states away // a song so
pungent // it rots
through the core of all his
bones // and still i await
to lap it up like a dog //
trained to drool at the
clean smashing of a bell //
it is his love that seeps out
of his pores // it is
contagious // it is a sick i
am willing to own

from the mouth of the Beehive

For Vincint

His mouth   a blushing rhythm of bees

spilling into   the queer

desert of eardrums

Can you hear it?

All that honey brown

burnt to the roof of his tongue

That way his black turns   butter

when   his gums open

Split like   dry folding dirt

in the small palms

of a glowing child

The boy listens to this   buzz on repeat

paints   himself   in a   glistening   pollen

He too knows   what it means
                  to be harvested for sap

A bruised Black   glitter hovering
              over rusting bone

A frail child, limbs glued on
backwards

To be a slick pane of glass
              jammed rigid into
the cathedral's   blistering tuff

How does molasses   continue to dance
once it's   lit on fire?
              This boy opens his jaws
vibrates   until all of the   windows
       shatter into a   raining cloud of dust
                  He names each flicker
                              of light his child
       as it pulls towards   our mouths
And   dances   wet   and loud

and new

Like a hive of   sugar being built   again

Unicorn Kidz Dance Under the Moonlight, Too

What is not soft here:

a boy spilling with glitter and gun oil

moon child moves like his mother's tides

a body that is all awkward and legs

we teach them to dance

then tell them it's not natural

to move their hips

what an image to be both

a thug nigga and a bitch nigga

what duality we shotgun into our stomach

grief knotting at the end of the spine

thug niggas ain't bitch niggas

don't be so soft

the streets will scrape

the cotton right out of you

they make a man out of anyone nowadays

boys sparkling like his grandma's gaudy earrings

dead fish limp wrist boy

dangling from the jaws of the block

left mangled and shimmering

in a rhinestone's blood

What is not soft here:

that cannot also be pierced by fangs

we stare the beast in the mouth

and dare it not to bite

dance around his tongue

and wait to be swallowed

my block will never love me back

not until I can produce a body made of less glitter

So what is not soft here:

that is not also dead

there has to be a place

for all us dead shining boys

i dream of a mother/not mine

contoured and glowing

kissing each one of our

foreheads and saying:

Black boy it's okay to dance

> *Black boy it's okay to dance*

Black boy it's okay to dance

> *Dance, black boy, dance*

They are no longer watching

It's okay, move your hips like the
crashing tide

Beast Boy

What animal will you transfix into today // Gaping hole fully ajar // Teeth strapling from your gums // as you smile // Skin crawling into a new shape // and you hide in all of this // Your friends know you // All green and musk // Tongue dragging from the side of your lip // A body full of bodies with more fur // And what is it to you // to assume the identity of another thing // You've been playing dress up // your entire life // I say you change animal // because the rest of the world won't believe // what we do is human // So we must be a beast/boy

Glisten

Every mouth in this club is a new glistening
home
        The music pulsating until the walls
become a fresh silt
dripping down the spines of every body present
        It isn't sweat
            But some sort of elixir
      they use in music videos to make
      everyone attractive in soaked
      movement
     This club is full of curve and flesh and
bad makeup
     but somehow we are all still
   beautiful
           Full of tequila
           and dancing to Whitney
           proclaiming she wants to
           dance with us
but doesn't know how
     Off to the side there are boys

clutching a brick background

moving hands up under each other's loose—

—fitting crop tops

                              Their tongues moisten

                    the already drenched air

the rest of us stare into the DJ booth

waiting for the next song to dive into

              And at some point the alcohol will take

over

                    We all try to find the shell of a

        body we can fit into like a tailored suit

              The music has to end soon

But at least we all leave the club soaking and smiling

Hide and Seek

It starts so simple—a boy
lost in a field, covered
in twigs, spread thick
to the fingertips. He learns
to play dead. How to still
his earthquaking chest
while others hive around
him in search—their loud
howls drifting towards
the timber in waiting. Most
of the others have all been
found and hung to dry
at the wrist by this point,
but this cannot end
until all of the faggots
have burned—childish game
they play. Who can spill the most
blood into the firepit to watch
the flames glow neon, how to
turn a boy into a blooming field

of flames. The art of hunting
with a lit torch and palms
full of gasoline, they continue
to scour. They cannot find
the boy. He stays hidden.

in defense of boys being bois

Maybe it is the black
heat of summer, its long

     freckling prongs forced
        into our anatomy, the hours

          of sun we choke down
            until we become light, so
        much

            that we only know
         how to run
              towards it,
            each scoopful of
            cosmic ray

doused in glitter
flickering in our windpipes. Maybe

it's the *bois* we wish we were.
    The muscle, the masculine, the unsick blood.

Painted silhouette of a cat's eye
        dressed in fool's gold foil. The
malleable

          tongue split into
          gender. Its bitter curl
            around a vile
          shaft.
            Dismemberment

and pickling of the *boi* body. Maybe
it's the way we are taught

to love, from a distance. The way we look
        at Terrell in gym class,

          his fresh pair of white shorts, Stephan
          running
            around the track, naked upper
          frame

          glistening in salt,
          Tyrone

and his

senior-bound

shoulders

bouldering in a thick brown skin.
When we are told to two-hand touch Johnny

in flag football and we try

not to let our hands slip

below his belt but we envision it

all later that night.
Our fingertips

tracing the

weight of his hem.
And

it's in the

language

of how we dream it; crawling

our fingers in between a boy's belt

loops, reaching into the unzipped fly
    of his Girbauds, pulling back a boy flocked

        in butterflies. Maybe it is just how we
are
           in sixth grade and have been
       taught

              we own nothing
                 including our
                own cauterized
                erection,

the dichotomy of the meat
    and what it is worth. Young us,

not yet understanding the soreness
    that thrashing bodies can bring.

        There is violence in every action,
           love is not the exception. We
       know

only of blood staining

the silk sheets

in our touch and I

guess

that is the simplest analogy

for currency. At eleven,

we have not yet learned

this form of division. We just know

the curvature of James'

still quaking abs and

if this is the price of

our cocooning body

being cracked

into a trickling cavity

by the blade of a boy's fearful hand
careening wildly into our sternum,

then bring on the light.

We welcome it.

Space

"...seasons where the cruel boys I chased and their

skinny sisters flamed and died in becoming..."

Audre Lorde ~ "Change of Season"

Unicorn Kid Comes Out to the Fraternity

On my twenty-fourth birthday I kissed a boy
like a descending ocean floor.
That night, we danced in a basement to
Die Young and *Starships* until we were
so drunk, our legs could not hold all the joy
sitting in our lungs. The music
was loud enough to end in a riot
cast of flung bricks. All we did that
night was smile. And laugh. And sing. And breathe.
Keep everything alive spinning clockwise.
I spent a whole summer in the darkest part
of a basement room at my dimly
lit fraternity house being a hushed Faggot.
But that night, we took back all
the crickets we could hide in our feet
and danced until their hum hit dawn.

On Jukin' wit a White Boy

After Jonah Mixon-Webster

The body is a collection of curves fleshy fat drenched
in the smell of sweat falling off it is programmed to
move toward the one and three of the others here have
asked to dance but I eyed you until your pupils told
me to come listen to my heartbeat let it guide your feet
should move this way back forth back forth right left
right left do you follow the trail of the rhythm once
stolen follows me into the muck of it all where my
hand grabs your hip and guides it like a wave in the
ocean drowning here I am still a black boy still in the
pit of the white still the exotic still the fresh meat
erection curdling the clean floor only accepted when a
pale winter boy took my hand to guide me to the open
shallow of the beast to throw me in

PReP

He asks me if I am on PReP
or why I am so careless with my own body
He has seen boys like me before
eager to ruin what little we have

I am drunk off my ass
and this man looks like an open field
or I look like open season
to these other older men

This is, after all,
The Chicago Jackhammer
where the men feast
on the young

But I am drunk and willing
to be a plate for any fist here
Surely, it is the sadness that brought me
to the table with an apple in my teeth

Notes on Cruising the Rest Stop off Exit 187 at 11:45 pm

The ritual is simple:

    Sit in the second stall

    Wait for the foot to spin

        the bottle towards you

    Three toe taps to testify

    the open jury joints

        of the knees ready for verdict

The act is easy:

    The shaft will slip its way into another

    This is where you hear

        a father's desire spill from a closet

    What a mess we've made of these throats

        trying to paint straight lines

    Waiting for the watchful hands

        to slide under the stall

            To say *come here my child,*

            I will hold you like I'm not able to my lover

    Let the symphony of sinks

        curtain closing themselves

        into a dry, wanting sky

Beware:

      of the attendants, or the officers,

      or the predators shaped like easy prey

If you're lucky:

      you'll end up alone,

         full of another man's semen

If you're lucky:

      you'll find a toe spun towards you

      A man that is not your father

         but will abuse you

just the same

The Art of Staying Alive

True, god did bid me sing but in the same breath did wish me death, and battle: a birthright to sing until emptied.

~ Marlin M. Jenkins, *Capable Monsters*

I claw open the boy and see his true
form. Light dripping out of a god's
body, wet and stale. He looks at me like how I did
when I first saw him. Like grease that bids
with the pot's skin; the boiling over that gambles me
dry. What faggot did not somersault out of their mother singing.
And that's it, we are used to our lovers causing us pain but
leaving us alive. Grinning from the back drenched in
honey. Sure he said he loved me, the
crooked way my lip hung from him. The same
way his ex would pull the iron from his breath.
Silly me to think he cared like I did.
To think he'd stretch out his sternum for me to make wishes
in between each licked bone. Piss-cleaned plate that held me
a bare meal waiting to be picked apart. A slow death
I guess, where there are a hundred mouths and
only one fork used to strip me. Lay my face down in the battle-

field. My arm stretched out, a

glorious pair of wings. I do not know if hurt is my birthright.

If I only choose men who will offer me to

hungrier men. Who shred me to the windpipe to hear me sing.

Call my voice beautiful until

my lungs collapse from being emptied.

Anatomy of the Jaw

Lessons on giving head

The bone breaks/splits at the back hinges
opens wide enough to swallow
a chicken whole/raw still
bleeding from the kill
meaning the uvula is still
coated in the fat of its last meal.
The way to a man's heart
is through his gutting/how much
of him you digest in a single sitting
It is through the slick slit
and how it hungers
to be filled/with him
it is never a question of when is dinner
rather where/and what limit
is he allowed to consume
But what a silly question
When we all know he cleans the plate
and takes the bones with him
when he leaves.

A Pantoum of Yellow Fields

For Tony

A field of yellow scatters the 1:00 AM community park
I am drunk therefore must be in love with you
The type of love that sticks to the back of the knees
midsummer and stays until the first fallen leaf

I am piss drunk off love for you
or the 5 shots of whiskey that smoke like
midsummer and stain the chest like drenched leaves
We roll around the dry grass, dogs shattering in heat

or the shots barreled into the moon still smoking
He asks if he could kiss me on the rough edge of my thigh
Roll around me like a field of shattered glass
and this time I am not too drunk to tell him yes

He asks if he could kiss my thighs like my ex used to
The type of love that sticks to the back of the knees
And this time I am not too drunk to tell him yes
To scatter myself bright yellow in this park at 1:00 AM

Let's Talk About Sex

a ghazal

He look at me like, you know, raised brows like it's *time for sex*
and he is curled smirk signaling you want to have sex

with me now, broad daylight in the middle of this Barnes and Noble
history section, next to the toys. Not sure why this flicks on his sex

drive, so I laugh, brush him off my shoulder, grab another book
but he says *come on, baby! That would be so hot, right? It's just sex!*

My own limbs dangling from the small link of his key—
—chain. Sure, in this act of conquest it could be "just sex"

or it could be my flesh pillaged again by foreign hands raking at my back
and I can feel it in the way his teeth kiss; the sweaty, twisted way the word, sex,

drops off his tongue. I hear the privilege bouncing around the space in his
throat when he says how much he loves me; *let's do it, let's fuck here, it's just sex.*

The Possum

It must be the way the meat opens

How it pours out like a shattering creak

The sparkle of blood

The glisten in the hot August air

The way it ferments in me

his kiss, wet as the backside of moss

How I lap up his cum with my ladled tongue

Most of my memories of him are like this

Sweat and flesh sealed close by a single sheet

It's how I wish to remember him always

in my arms, his skin pressed against my bone

Maybe it's the way he guts me like a possum does its roadkill/The deer with its jaw splattered rolling down the highway and the possum fishing through its remains for his next meal/I don't blame him for taking what he needs to survive/the lungs and all/It is in our nature to find comfort in the blood of others

It must be the   open

                pour

                        of blood

The   hot August

                ferments in

his kiss

                his   tongue

                memories

                        close

                                always

                pressed against my bone

                it's the way he guts me

                                for his next meal/I don't blame

                                        the

nature   of others

                the way the meat

sparkles

glistens

wet

How   my   tongue

remembers him

pressed against

the lungs

It must be

in the blood

Notes on Sucking Dick at the DC Eagle During Pride

the bouncer at the front door   is a breaking comet   hands
stapled into fractured glass   carefully counter-clicking my entering
  as if to say how much   he noticed my open mouth
  as I walked in telling me   what he would do   with its crystal
ball glisten
soft sheen

but i am probably overthinking his gratitude   imagine: his towering
cock a pillar of   soft sand   inside me

:::

 i stir the ice in the glass   until it starts to crack offer it my
warm lip as a piece of solace   i know what it is like to be
forced   into smaller   divisions
of the body   considered only for how well   i can fit in someone's
jaw

:::

i am here only for the music   for the empty   associated with large

clubs   and   muscle bears   to be able to say i went

   where the boys

found me

irresistible and i made it out alive

:::

that none of the boys here   are worth my time   by that i mean

        i have felt the violence   these boys keep in their pants

        and not once has my chest split open

at the seam   of the sternum   for that I can only be grateful

        that the man across the bar   did not rip me open

leave the remains of my stomach fuming   from the swine's end

        did not make the bathroom floor   my burial when i traveled

                to take a piss   how i watched him watch me bottom jaw agape

                at my slow release   how he followed me to the

patio   i knew   my teeth   would be found

stitched into the sandstone

:::

another man touches me at the bar and i can feel my lungs shattering

climbing   my esophagus   bejeweled   gloss

fractals   of my spine left by men who only offer me options keep this

body a doorway   to a morgue   laughing at my throat

          there are so many men here

that could want me dead

and i carelessly walked into a club

without considering   the eyes who only saw me
readied to spill out dirt   become a hole   left only for

their entering

:::

Boystown

I go to boystown; lay naked in the middle of the street and wait for a car to hit me and isn't that just my life? Waiting for things to come ruin me; boi laid stretched out on the bed or road or the bathroom stall, ready to be destroyed inside out. I will marvel at this wreckage. The body pried from the mouth of the car, split in two clean halves down the middle. Open bloodied and grinning. And it doesn't have to be the gay district of Chicago, it could be New York or DC or Los Angeles or my home I just happened to be here when my body decided it needed to be turned to dust and it's funny, the miracles we create when we don't want them, middle of the day and busy street but no cars came to level me, so instead I found a boy to do the shoveling, I wonder if he knows what he's buried.

A Sonnet for the Woods Behind St. Joseph Mercy Hospital

Sneak into the small forest off Golfside
road. The boy on your phone tells you to meet
him at the browning thicket in the zipped
mouthed trees. You are sure the thin black fog will

be your undoing. A man made of beard
and blank face asking you to find him at
the corner of nowhere and missing. Scared
and horny you go. Trample through the soft

leaves left soiled by the beasts hidden in bark
sap. The July humidity clings to
your shirt like an ex-lover. A night sky
filled with scratching dirt and twitching twigs. Piles

of faggots waiting to be lit under
the moon's soft glow. You find this boy——opened.

A Duplex for the Boy with the Cool Blue Truck in Pennsylvania

I am terrified of the backroads hanging off Pennsylvania.
A boy asks me to meet him in the dark alley of a country woods.

       The boy asks me to ravage him on the creaking off-trail road,
       carve my name in him and with that I'd stay forever.

Carve my skin with his and become a glass jar for now.
I share my location with my best friend of where to find me.

       I share my body with a boy and only my best friend knows
       where I hide when my skin is unlatching at the armpits and ankles.

Where I hide all bodies blooming in the swirl of my gut.
But his palms requested me, the small bleeding prize he can hold

       in his hands. A trophy bleeding out always at his request.
       And sure, I am afraid this man in my cell is a murderer

or that this white man might be racist and I am unknowing.
I am terrified of being found hanging off the Pennsylvania backroads.

Unicorn Kid Loves to Worship Grief

And what other parts of the tongue do we owe
grief? Once I met a boy and this is how

the story always begins. Cupped in the scathing
fur of desolate men; found in a bed I cannot help

but sink in, wedged in between his bladed
teeth. The way he holds my name like a knife

to my throat. And I will call this *love.* Name this
man I've known for 12 hours, via a phone app*,*

a new set of lungs. Surprised when he leaves and all
of a sudden I cannot breathe. This must be *grief*

or *love.* There is a list of men drawn in my spit.
I will never be able to untaste them and that too

is a form of *grief.* When we call on gravity
to pull us back to its chest, forgetting

the splitting of the boi upon brute
impact. Silly boy and all his buckling

knees. The way gravel is permanently lodged
into the tibula. The way I ask for the shredding

of my own skin before I ask for mercy. A boy
begs me to spit my salt into his mouth

and I do, wipe what I missed leaking
on his cheek with my finger and drop it

on his gums and I pretend that this too is *love*.
The same *love* a 13 year old boy gives himself

as he scours the internet to find an image
of two men kissing in order to empty

himself. The same *grief* I look for in the back alleys
of gay bars and the restrooms of truck stops.

The same *love* souring the pig-fat
of my windpipe as I prepare another man,

another plot of dirt clawed open by my drying
inheritance. The same *love*

I was taught in the back of my church
praying myself new:

Oh god
Oh holy god
I forgot who I was supposed to *worship*

Reality

"There are only so many parallel universes

that concern us.   In one, he isn't dead."

Franny Choi ~ "Introduction to Quantum Theory"

Debt:

i am learning/to be a Good *Boi*

for you/no matter how many tries it takes

I.

–tucked underneath the plush, swelling comforters, you ask what is my favorite part of you. This question of sectioning bodies. Compartmentalizations of what to keep, of what we wish could be discarded. The same way your mother divides your bed into two equal parts by a long, beige blanket tucked down the middle when I would spend the night.

She does not know we share the same sheet while we rest, your head cratered into my chest. Or that I know the smell of you at 3am, tongue driven up your spine. You are the first boy to touch my queering body like I'm supposed to keep breathing. The currency of my jaw is just a way to repay that debt–

I will forever owe you for your ash-slick hands, for the light of your morning breath, for the tiny forts

we laid in built out of our slow growing pubic
hair, for your silence–

–Everyone leaves at some point, most by way of ghost. I have so many specters following at this point, I must be my own seance. I am dressed in full sequins and a man on the street corner calls me a *faggot*–I hear only the voice of the last man I let love my body the wrong way. I find a boy on an app and allow him into my home in hopes that he intends on hurting me–

II.

–At five, I roll on the floor near my mother's feet. I tell her I do not wish to die, she says to me too bad, we all will. This is in the wake of her mother's mother's funeral. Ever since, I've been so unafraid of leaving. We are machines built of time and letting go. I guess leaving this earth is just me settling my debt with god, he gave me a body and sins and blood and desire and let me fuck who I wanted, even when others told me I should die for it. So I guess leaving a man who loves me too well is me settling my own debt. I never returned to my mother to ask how she was coping with her grandmother's death–

–I must ask how much my slow death was worth. A single grin cut across my casket; small mouth spilling out gold coins in its rot. How much of me was spent in the making of you. This universe where you are the brightest star set to implode in on itself–

–my skin/my skin/my skin/my skin/my
skin/my skin/my skin/my skin/my skin/my
skin/my skin/my skin/my skin/my skin/my
skin/my skin/my skin/my skin/my skin/my
skin/my skin/my skin/my skin/my skin/my
skin/my skin/my skin/my skin/my skin/my
skin/my skin/my skin/my skin/my skin/my
skin/my skin/my skin/my skin/my skin/my
skin/my skin/my skin/my skin/my skin/my
skin/my skin/my skin/my skin/my skin/my
skin/my skin/my skin/my skin/my skin/my
skin/my skin/my skin/my skin/my skin/my
skin/my skin/my skin/my skin/my skin/my
skin/my skin/my skin/my skin/my skin/my
skin/my skin/my skin/my skin/my skin/my
skin/my sin/my sin/my sin/my sin/my sin/my
sin/my sin/my sin/my sin/my sin/my sin/my
sin/my sin/my sin/my sin/my sin/my sin/my
sin/my sin/my sin/my sin/my sin/my sin/my
sin/my sin/my sin/my sin/my sin/my sin/my
sin/my sin/my sin/my sin/my sin/my sin/my
sin/my sin/my sin/my sin/my sin/my sin/my

sin/my sin/my sin/my sin/my sin/my sin/my
sin/my sin/my sin/my sin/my sin/my sin/my
sin/my sin/my sin/my sin/my sin/my sin/my
sin/my sin/my sin/my sin/my sin/my sin/my
sin/my sin/my sin/my sin/my sin/my sin/my–

—again I speak of violence like it is owed to me.
I could fill a ledger with debt, I would never
know how to repay it. Life is not long enough
to settle our tabs with our loves, let them spill
over into the next one—

III.

–I've only understood violence by way of
compromise. How I find the pike driven
through the bottom of my glossed skull left
displayed at the base of a man's bed. There are
so many things I'm unsure of, including wrath,
it's debt to my skin. I think about the Grief I
have offered allowance, space at my table, a
good, warm meal.

I'm not sure if I give it what's it's owed, just
what I think is due. I exchange my teeth for
happiness and then I forget how to smile with
my whole mouth. I forget the color of my
glistening gums–

–tell me to go and I'll go. I'm not sure why I'm
stuck here. I understand leaving, the creation of

space between two bodies of wet salt. I think of that one meme of the fish late to work because Moses split the Red Sea to create safe passage for his people. I wonder what lovers were forever split in the act of saving.

I wonder who searched on the other side of that chasm to find their love drowned or to not find them at all. If a wall fell between me and my love, I don't know if I'd climb it for him. I don't know if I trust a man not willing to leave–

–in fourth grade, I liked a boy so much that I
only knew how to make fun of his shoes. A year
later, the same boy kicked dirt in my eyes during
recess and I thanked him. And O the simple *I
Love You* that would not suffice, I would gladly
claw out my lover's heart and gift it to them.
The violence of love on repeat, I ask what is your
favorite part of me, take it for yourself and care
to it like a wound you don't want to heal–

–boys are so wrong so often, especially about lust; especially when there is another boi involved learning their own mutant flesh. What is love? What is conquering the country of piled hands? What is all this sharing of what I have no right to own? Who am I to deny someone the space on my tongue–

IV.

—I was once owned by a boy and all I received
in return was his guilt. Such a concept, the
property of lust. How we long so much to
own something, let it be the boi poured from
a lover's cement. Halpern states, "this eternity
of stars repeating, whatever you make me
swallow, I'll swallow," and in this I imagine
you, again in my mouth, a stone turned over
by my tongue until it is drenched in my spit
and carried down my esophagus. Please tell
me what I owe you, so I can settle and forget;

memory is another form of
debt—

–I cannot think of debt without thinking of my own inheritance, of what has been gifted, all of it's costs. My mother's aching joints, my father's temper.

The thrashing caused by my blood when a boy slaps the back of my scalp in the name of love. I have asked for so much to be bestowed, I fear my greed will be rewarded one day with everything it requests.

A bladed hand swift to the back of my neck. A boy built from spit and mud and a handful of daggers pointed at my chest. A lullaby that foretells my own unraveling at the swirling of it's softest notes tucked tight coiling my neck.

I find no space safe for a queer boi to live on this already dying planet. How often I wonder how I inherited such a thing, all this hurt, all these sticks I wish would burn–

V.

–I have watched your mother split your bed
into two at least a hundred times over; and in
my mind, I know you think of this as the
fractioning of your own flesh. She must know
something, the way she brings in a sleeping bag
and extra pillows, the extra knock on the door
to ensure we are not just skin and sweat, the
hush in your silhouette as we dance around the
questions. How did you boys sleep? What time
did you get to bed? You both were so quiet,
how are you both always so quiet–

—the answer to your question has always been caught in between the stale rot of our kiss. Behind the bite, your mother calls me your best friend in public and you call me your boyfriend in private and I am neither/I am both. I am a wick slow burning at each end and I revel in it; this waxy death. Maybe that is just the grease of greed slick with want. The answer to your question is you and is not you. My favorite part might be the Grief I collect to fill the empty space you leave—

VI.

−to be lipstick and ass and cinched waist
bruising my liver. To be enough good woman
for him to stay another night. I dream of it, legs
wrapped in the best part of the bacon. Tits
perked and laying across his chest. I am what he
dreams of, a body left safe for consumption. I
always wake again in this boy body, the boi
bursting from the seams−

–There is a thicket of evergreen growing at the brim of my stomach. I pick finely at its spruces letting them brown out at my feet. You planted them for me, a small forest of want. Lush greenery shuffling in my gut. I wish to hold you there like potted shrubbery sprouting into my intestines. "Whatever you make me swallow, I'll swallow" even you, or just the sum of your pulsating cock made cedar in me. Or maybe just a juniper sweet, your sap syrups its way down my palms–

–I guess the real question is what am I doing? Why all this reimagined past carved from zombie rot–flesh? What dead love am I trying to conjure from their faux grave? I remember a poem by Franny Choi that speaks of a multiverse that holds you in it; maybe a different you, but still sad. I'm just questioning what universe I would choose if given back the magic. The one where my lover—hand sculpted by my lust—has a pulse and a new man. The one where I get to watch my lover die in my arms over and over, replayed in the tape deck of my cornea. The one where the boy tells me he loves me and turns into a gust of leaves sweeping out the front door.

I have found no reality where the boy remains mine. I can make another and another until I carve out the one I want. I don't care the cost.

Notes

"Let's Talk about Sex" shares a title with the Salt-N-Pepa.

"On Jukin' wit a White Boy" is after "On Jukin' wit a Black Boy" by Jonah Mixon-Webster; a poem for Danez Smith.

"From the mouth of the Beehive" is made in response to Vincint's "Hard 2 Forget."

"Beast Boy" is based on the DC comic book Character that shares the same name.

"The Art of Staying Alive" is a Golden Shovel written after lines in a poem in *Capable Monsters* called "Pokedex Entry #39: Jigglypuff."

"Debt" is based on Franny Choi's poem "Introduction to Quantum Theory" and borrows a line from Rob Halpern's poem "A Square, A Cell, A Sentence."

Thank You Notes

Dear Reader,

Thank you first. The fact that you picked up this book means you believe in my work or you really liked the cover art, but either way, I hope this was a wild ride you are willing to try again. Thank you always to my mother, you are a guiding light in my everyday life! Thank you Jamie, for being my biggest supporter and an amazing little sister.

Thank you to my newest little sister Taylor, for editing this book first, for believing in me always, championing other's work and words, for letting me FaceTime you for no reason other than to talk mess, you have truly been a blessing. Thank you Jihyun, for looking over this chapbook and telling me it was a full length, you were right! It means a lot to me that you are so willing and kind.

Thank you to Michelle and David, my last line of editing defense and huge supporters of mine, I have thrown this book away at least 12 times but you always stop me. Thank you Ellen, I can truly say you are like my poetry mother, it means the world to me!

Thank you The Knight's Library staff for putting up with me and keeping me in check, that has nothing to do with this book but I felt it was important. Thank you MMPR Collective, you are an amazing soundboard, I appreciate the edits, the congrats, the love, the care, you all are my second family.

Thank you to Sundress, to Erin, to SAFTA, to everyone that works so hard in publishing these wonderful collections. Your words, foresight, generosity, willingness to work through the work, and the fact that you put up with me for months of being early for literally everything because I am annoying. Thank you mostly for believing that my work has value and needs to be placed in the world. There is so much I have learned in this process because of you all.

Thank you to my local venues, Skazat! and Ann Arbor Poetry for allowing me to test the water with some of these poems, also for being the first ever open mics I ever went to. I don't know if my poetry would be the same without you.

Thank you Eastern Michigan University Creative Writing program for making me switch to poetry even though I said I was a fiction writer, specifically Rob who stood me up in the middle of the class to force me to read my weird poem because I had finally did what you were trying to make me do, I have been doing it ever since. Thank you to Jonah, Lannie, Eric, and so many others who walked with me on this journey.

Thank you YpsiArbor, DC, Lansing, and Toledo. Each one of you is represented in this collection, I hope I did you proud. Special shoutout to Rest Stops and Shady Parks, you helped me create this content.

Much Love
jason

About the Author

jason b. crawford (they/them) is a writer born in Washington DC, raised in Lansing, MI. Their debut chapbook collection, *Summertime Fine,* is out through Variant Lit. Their second chapbook, *Twerkable Moments*, is out from Paper Nautilus Press. Their third chapbook, *Good Boi*, was released by Neon Hemlock Press in Fall 2021.

Crawford holds a Bachelor of Science in Creative Writing from Eastern Michigan University and is the co-founder of *The Knight's Library Magazine*. Crawford is the winner of the Courtney Valentine Prize for Outstanding Work by a Millennial Artist, Vella Chapbook Contest, and Variant Lit Chapbook Contest. They are the 2021 OutWrite chapbook contest winner in poetry. Their work can be found in *Split Lip Magazine, Glass Poetry, Four Way Review, Voicemail Poems, FreezeRay Poetry, HAD*, among others. They are a current poetry MFA candidate at The New School.

Other Sundress Titles

Slaughter the One Bird
Kimberly Ann Priest
$16

Dad Jokes from Late in the Patriarchy
Amorak Huey
$16

The Valley
Esteban Rodriguez
$16

What Nothing
Anna Meister
$16

To Everything There Is
Donna Vorreyer
$16

Hood Criatura
féi hernandez
$16

nightsong
Ever Jones
$16

Maps of Injury
Chera Hammons
$16

www.ingramcontent.com/pod-product-compliance
Lightning Source LLC
Chambersburg PA
CBHW081234090426
42738CB00016B/3306